Alaska
ALPHABET
and
NUMBERS
Book

by Doug Lindstrand

First U.S. Edition, October, 1986

ABCDEFGHIJKLMNOPQRSTUVWXYZ

ABCDEF
GHIJKL
MNOPQ
RSTUV
WXYZ

Ten 10

Add

$$9 + 1 = 10$$
$$5 + 5 = 10$$

Subtract

$$10 - 0 = 10$$

Multiply

$$10 \times 1 = 10$$
$$5 \times 2 = 10$$

0 1 2 3 4 5 6 7 8 9 10

Alaska is known as America's "Last Frontier." It is the largest state, the one with the highest mountains and one of the most beautiful places in the world. So if you live in Alaska or are just visiting, please don't litter or feed the wild animals.
Thank you,
Snowball and Snowflake Polar Bear

Eight 8

Add

$$7 + 1 = 8$$
$$4 + 4 = 8$$

Subtract

$$10 - 2 = 8$$
$$9 - 1 = 8$$

Multiply

$$8 \times 1 = 8$$
$$4 \times 2 = 8$$

0 1 2 3 4 5 6 7 8 9 10

Nine 9

Add

$$8 + 1 = 9$$

$$5 + 4 = 9$$

Subtract

$$10 - 1 = 9$$

$$9 - 0 = 9$$

Multiply

$$9 \times 1 = 9$$

$$3 \times 3 = 9$$

0 1 2 3 4 5 6 7 8 9 10

ABCDEFGHIJKLMNOPQRSTUVWXYZ
abcdefghijklmnopqrstuvwxyz

Bb

Bzzzzzzzzz

"B" words: Brown bear, bee, balloons, berries, basket and bushes.

ABCDEFGHIJKLMNOPQRSTUVWXYZ
abcdefghijklmnopqrstuvwxyz

C c

Caribou chewing colorful cookies.

ABCDEFGHIJKLMNOPQRSTUVWXYZ
abcdefghijklmnopqrstuvwxyz

d

D

"D" words: **D**all ram, **d**og, **d**eer and **d**aisies.

ABCD**E**FGHIJKLMNOPQRSTUVWXYZ
abcd**e**fghijklmnopqrstuvwxyz

E

"E" words: Eagles, Eskimos and Easter eggs.

ABCDEFGHIJKLMNOPQRSTUVWXYZ
abcdefghijklmnopqrstuvwxyz

Ff

"F" words: Fox, fire, frog, Alaska flag and flowers.

ABCDEFGHIJKLMNOPQRSTUVWXYZ
abcdefghijklmnopqrstuvwxyz

G g

Goose, goat and gold nuggets in green grass.

ABCDEFGHIJKLMNOPQRSTUVWXYZ
abcdefghijklmnopqrstuvwxyz

h

B·z·z·z·z·z
B·z·z·z·z

H

B·z·z·z·z·z

"H" words: Huskies, hamburgers, hot dogs, hive, heart and honey jar.

ABCDEFGHIJKLMNOPQRSTUVWXYZ
abcdefghijklmnopqrstuvwxyz

"I" words: Iceberg, igloo, ice cream and ice cubes.

ABCDEFGHIJKLMNOPQRSTUVWXYZ
abcdefghijklmnopqrstuvwxyz

"J" words: Jack-o-lantern, jelly, jam, jars and jet.

ABCDEFGHIJKLMNOPQRSTUVWXYZ
abcdefghijklmnopqrstuvwxyz

"K" words: King salmon, kite, kittens and kissing.

"L" words: Lynx kitten, lightning and lupine flowers.

ABCDEFGHIJKLMNOPQRSTUVWXYZ
abcdefghijklmnopqrstuvwxyz

Little lambs leaping over log cabin.

ABCDEFGHIJKLMNOPQRSTUVWXYZ
abcdefghijklmnopqrstuvwxyz

Musher meeting muskox and mouse in mountains.

ABCDEFGHIJKLMNOPQRSTUVWXYZ
abcdefghijklmnopqrstuvwxyz

"N" words: Nest, numbers, north, nails and gold nuggets.

ABCDEFGHIJKLMNOPQRSTUVWXYZ
abcdefghijklmnopqrstuvwxyz

"O" words: **O**ctopus, **o**cean, **o**wls, **o**il pipeline and **o**ld tree.

ABCDEFGHIJKLMNOPQRSTUVWXYZ
abcdefghijklmnopqrstuvwxyz

"P" words: Polar bear, porcupine, ptarmigan, purple pig, pancakes, pumpkin pie, puddle and pails of popcorn.

"Q" words: Quiver, quarter of cake, porcupine quills, quart of milk and question mark.

ABCDEFGHIJKLMNOPQRSTUVWXYZ
abcdefghijklmnopqrstuvwxyz

Rabbit resting on rock with red rose.

r

"R" words: Robins, rainbow, rope and rubber tire.

Sourdough and squirrels on snowy slope.

ABCDEFGHIJKLMNOPQRSTUVWXYZ
abcdefghijklmnopqrstuvwxyz

Ss

"S" words: Snowman, sun, swan, stocking hat and scarf.

ABCDEFGHIJKLMNOPQRSTUVWXYZ
abcdefghijklmnopqrstuvwxyz

T t

"T" words: Twin cubs, two, toys, tulips and trees.

ABCDEFGHIJKLMNOPQRSTUVWXYZ
abcdefghijklmnopqrstuvwxyz

U

u

Under umbrellas.

ABCDEFGHIJKLMNOPQRSTUVWXYZ
abcdefghijklmnopqrstuvwxyz

Viewing erupting volcanoes.

ABCDEFGHIJKLMNOPQRSTUVWXYZ
abcdefghijklmnopqrstuvwxyz

Wolf, walrus and whale at waterfall.

ABCDEFGHIJKLMNOPQRSTUVWXYZ
abcdefghijklmnopqrstuvwxyz

Bear playing **X**ylophone.

X

"**X**" marks the treasure map.

ABCDEFGHIJKLMNOPQRSTUVWXYZ
abcdefghijklmnopqrstuvwxyz

"Y"

words: Yawning fox, yo-yo and yellow sun.

ABCDEFGHIJKLMNOPQRSTUVWXYZ
abcdefghijklmnopqrstuvwxyz

"Z" words: Zippers, zero degrees and zero number.

NUMBERS

0–10

01234567 8910

0 Zero	6 Six
1 One	7 Seven
2 Two	8 Eight
3 Three	9 Nine
4 Four	10 Ten
5 Five	

Zero 0

Add

$$0 + 0 = 0$$

Subtract

$$2 - 2 = 0$$
$$1 - 1 = 0$$

Multiply

$$0 \times 0 = 0$$

0 1 2 3 4 5 6 7 8 9 10

One 1

Add

$$1 + 0 = 1$$

Subtract

$$3 - 2 = 1$$
$$2 - 1 = 1$$

Multiply

$$1 \times 1 = 1$$

0 1 2 3 4 5 6 7 8 9 10

Two 2

Add

$$2 + 0 = 2$$
$$1 + 1 = 2$$

Subtract

$$4 - 2 = 2$$
$$3 - 1 = 2$$

Multiply

$$2 \times 1 = 2$$

0 1 2 3 4 5 6 7 8 9 10

Three 3

Add

$$3 + 0 = 3$$
$$2 + 1 = 3$$

Subtract

$$5 - 2 = 3$$
$$4 - 1 = 3$$

Multiply

$$3 \times 1 = 3$$

0 1 2 3 4 5 6 7 8 9 10

Four 4

Add

$$3 + 1 = 4$$
$$2 + 2 = 4$$

Subtract

$$6 - 2 = 4$$
$$5 - 1 = 4$$

Multiply

$$4 \times 1 = 4$$
$$2 \times 2 = 4$$

0 1 2 3 4 5 6 7 8 9 10

Five 5

Add

$$4 + 1 = 5$$
$$3 + 2 = 5$$

Subtract

$$7 - 2 = 5$$
$$6 - 1 = 5$$

Multiply

$$5 \times 1 = 5$$

0 1 2 3 4 5 6 7 8 9 10

Six 6

Add				
5	+	1	=	6
3	+	3	=	6

Subtract				
8	−	2	=	6
7	−	1	=	6

Multiply				
6	×	1	=	6
3	×	2	=	6

0 1 2 3 4 5 6 7 8 9 10

Seven 7

Add

$$6 + 1 = 7$$
$$4 + 3 = 7$$

Subtract

$$9 - 2 = 7$$
$$8 - 1 = 7$$

Multiply

$$7 \times 1 = 7$$

0 1 2 3 4 5 6 7 8 9 10